LMS
Branch Lines
1945 ~ 65

Blackwell Mill, Derbyshire, situated in the triangle between Miller's Dale Junction and the Buxton branch of the former Midland Railway was for many years claimed by the LMS as the 'smallest station in Britain', a claim that is open to dispute. The platforms were provided for railway staff who lived in cottages inside the triangle of lines and had no access to a public highway. The LMS gratuitously provided the platforms for their staff to enable them to get to Buxton for shopping and other necessities. The Midland 0-6-0 with a mixed freight waits for the road to Buxton at a fine Midland semaphore signal.

Crown Copyright National Railway Museum, York.

LMS
Branch Lines
1945 ~ 65

by C.J. Gammell

Oxford Publishing Co.

SBN 86093 062 9

Printed by
B.H. Blackwell Ltd. in the City of Oxford

ACKNOWLEDGEMENTS

The author and publisher would like to acknowledge the help given by T.J. Edgington of the National Railway Museum, Neville Dexter for photographic services, C.H.A. Townley for valuable research assistance and 'Dolores' for typing the manuscript. The following photographs were taken by the individuals and organisations shown and much help is appreciated in this respect.

T J Edgington: 2, 3
National Railway Museum: 9, 11, 28, 30, 31, 76, 79
C H A Townley: 4, 10, 12, 15, 18, 22, 23, 27, 29, 33–37, 39, 40, 42, 44, 47, 49, 50, 55, 58, 63, 67, 68, 74, 75, 80, 81, 83, 85, 94, 97, 101, 105, 133
E Wilmshurst: 19–21, 25, 26, 32, 64, 77, 78, 84, 106, 108, 115, 119, 125
Lens of Sutton: 53, 54, 114, 118, 122, 147, 157, 158
L & GRP: 1, 16, 43, 48, 73, 91–3, 136, 137
J H Meredith: 111
H C Casserley: 82, 110, 134, 154, 155

Published by
Oxford Publishing Co.
8 The Roundway
Headington
Oxford

Contents

Bibliography

British Branch Lines H A Vallance — *Batsford 1965*

The Railways of Wharfedale P E Bangham — *D & C 1969*

The North Staffordshire Railway R Christiansen & R W Miller — *D & C 1971*

The Furness Railway R W Rush — *Oakwood 1973*

Passengers No More G Daniels & L Dench — *Ian Allan 1973*

Regional History of the Railways of Great Britain Vol. 7 Rex Christiansen — *D & C 1973*

Locomotives at The Grouping Vol. 3 H C Casserley & S W Johnson — *Ian Allan 1974*

Regional History of the Railways of Great Britain Vol. 8 David Joy — *D & C 1975*

Regional History of the Railwavs of Great Britain Vol. 9 Robin Leleux — *D & C 1976*

Rail Atlas of Britain S Baker — *OPC 1977*

Closed Railway Lines in Britain N J Hill & A D McDougall — *B.L.S. 1977*

Leicester & Swannington Railway C R Clinker — *A.A.A. 1977*

Regional History of the Railways of Great Britain Vol. 10 Geoffrey Holt — *D & C 1978*

Introduction

The London Midland & Scottish Railway, created in 1923 out of the 1921 Railways Act was the largest of the 'four' main line companies in Britain. The branch lines came from the constituent companies of the LMS, the Midland, LNWR, L & Y, Caledonian, GSWR, NSR and Highland plus a few minor companies which were absorbed at the same time in the 'grouping'. The LMS did not have much money to spend on branch lines and these, like the minor lines of the other companies, suffered severe loss of patronage with the rise of motor car ownership and the establishment of efficient bus routes. The LMS did a lot to standardise its locomotive fleet and many branch lines were fortunate enough to have modern motive power, even if the stations were old fashioned. Sometimes a pre-grouping ticket would be discovered or a rack full of old luggage labels headed by the pre-1923 company's name—such was the neglect in which some of the stations were found. The LMS and its successor the London Midland Region, was very much the 'main line' railway, and branch lines, although seriously starved of capital, were always 'part of the system', even if they were remote and had meagre services. LMS branch lines north of the border are not included in this book as they have been adequately covered in *Scottish Branch Lines 1955–1965*, a companion book in the same series. Much has been written about the famous Stanier Pacifics, West Coast expresses and high speed trains, but little notice has been taken of the minor byways with slow trains, picturesque countryside, a leisurely pace of life, staff able to pass the time of day and old fashioned stations—a way of life now alas no longer with us.

LONDON   *C. J. Gammell*
March 1980

Bacup, a Lancashire branch line terminus served by two lines. A Class 2 2-6-0 about to depart on the 17.30 to Manchester Victoria with LMS coaches in early BR cream and red livery in an April shower.

5 April, 1952

Abbreviations Used

LMS	London Midland & Scottish Railway
LNWR	London & North Western Railway
L&YR	Lancashire & Yorkshire Railway
NSR	North Stafford Railway
NLR	North London Railway
GSWR	Glasgow & South Western Railway

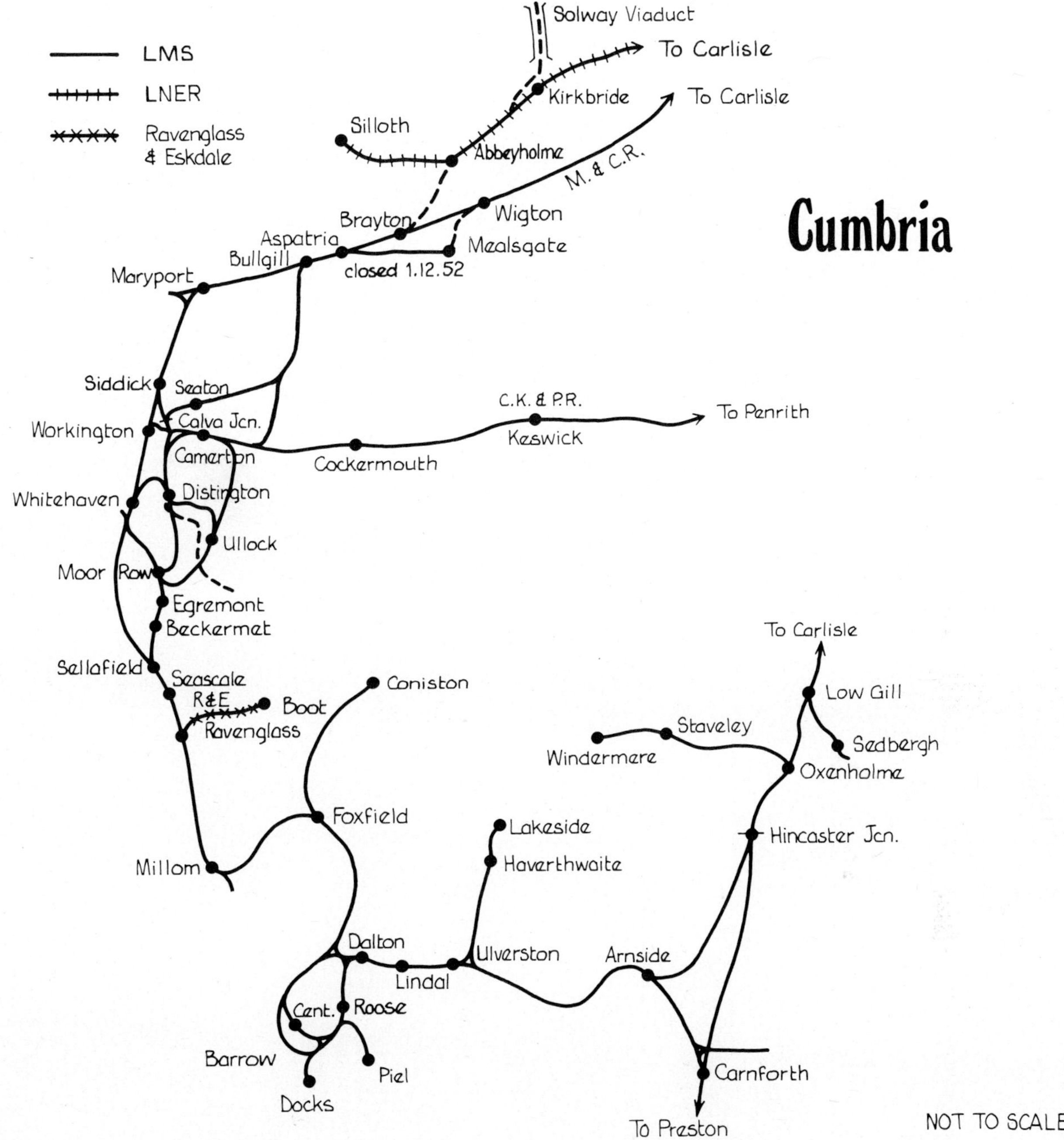

The Lake District of England was served by the Cockermouth, Keswick and Penrith Railway, the Furness Railway and the London & North Western Railway. The industrial region around Workington and Whitehaven supplied the area with coal, iron ore and steel. The Caledonian Railway even arrived on the scene by building a direct line over the Solway Firth and running over the Maryport & Carlisle Railway. The mineral traffic, for which the line was built, declined and the Solway Viaduct was finally demolished in 1935. Regular steam running in the summer months over the Furness main line from Carnforth to Sellafield was reintroduced in 1978. A curious connecting line on the Furness system was that from Hincaster to Arnside, opened on 26 June, 1876, closed to passengers 1 March, 1953 and closed to all traffic on 9 September, 1963, although Sandside to Arnside lasted until 1 January, 1972.

1. **A fine study of Threlkeld** station of the former Cockermouth, Keswick and Penrith Railway, looking towards Keswick showing the island platform, goods dock and LNWR type signals. Passenger services were withdrawn from Penrith to Keswick on 6 March, 1972 and Keswick to Workington on 18 April, 1966. Freight services were withdrawn from Penrith to Blencow on 19 June, 1972, Blencow to Keswick on 6 March, 1972 and Workington on 18 April, 1966.

1 August, 1949

2. Moor Row, a Cumberland junction, with a Class 4F 0-6-0 on an Egremont to Workington train in April 1950. This was probably the school train, as the regular passenger service from Sellafield to Whitehaven finished on 16 April, 1947. School trains ran until 3 March, 1969. The line is still open for freight traffic. The section from Beckermet to Sellafield closed to all traffic on 19 January, 1970. The passenger service from Moor Row to Camerton and Siddick ceased on 13 April, 1931, freight traffic to Camerton finished on 19 November, 1960 and to Distington on 1 July, 1963.

3. In September 1954 Class 2 tank
No 41217 stands at Coniston, a
lakeland terminus of the former
Furness Railway. Note the cast
iron seats on the platform with
the squirrel in the ironwork.
These seats were very numerous
on the Furness system—some are
now preserved at York Museum.
Passenger services were withdrawn on 6 October, 1958 and
the line closed to all traffic
on 30 April, 1962.

4. Barrow Shipyard had a passenger
service (unadvertised) for work-
men and this picture shows a
Class 4 2-6-4T about to work the
07.45 to Millom. The line closed
to all traffic with effect from
3 July, 1967. The nearby branch
to Piel closed on 6 July, 1936.

31 August, 1954

5. Windermere, a busy branch in the Lake District with heavy motive power in use. A 'Britannia' Class 7 4-6-2 arrives on the excursion, probably from Blackpool, in August 1964. The signal posts are of LNWR origin as well as the signal box.

6. No 42154, a 2-6-4T allocated to Carnforth (shown on the buffer beam) arrives at Staveley, on the Windermere branch with a stopping passenger train to Oxenholme. Note the peculiar passenger head code with oil lamp offset, as there is no top bracket for the lamp. The water is spilling over the top of the tanks, as the train is being brought to a stand too quickly. The first coaches are of LNER origin. Note the LNWR use of timber in the platform construction. The branch is still open.

7. In the summer of 1960 an SLS/MLS rail-tour has arrived at Lakeside, now operated by the short Lakeside & Haverthwaite Railway. Passengers disembarked here from the train straight onto the steamers, which plied on nearby Lake Windermere seen in the background. The Lakeside line closed on 26 September, 1938 to regular traffic but summer excursions lasted until 6 September, 1965. Ulverston to Haverthwaite closed to all traffic on 24 April, 1967. The section onwards from Haverthwaite to Lakeside is now operated by the Lakeside & Haverthwaite Railway, a preserved railway using ex-LMS locomotives in various colours.

8. Sedbergh, on the Tebay to Clapham branch, showing the solid structure common to the stations on the line using the stone materials from local quarries. Although passenger services were withdrawn on the Low Gill to Clapham line on 1 February, 1954, this route continued to be used for many years for diversion, especially on Sundays when heavy engineering work was in progress on either the ex-Midland main line or the ex-LNWR from Carlisle. The branch closed to all traffic on 19 June, 1966.
21 August, 1965

Lancashire, Greater Manchester and Merseyside

The North West of England saw the construction of the 'first main line', from Liverpool to Manchester in 1830, soon followed by branch lines and inter-connections, for the area was to become a labyrinth of railways. The LNWR, L&YR and Cheshire Lines rivalled one another for the Liverpool—Manchester traffic. In North Lancs the L&Y held away and had some choice branch lines in industrial areas and even on the edge of the Pennines, served by push and pull trains developed from the steam 'railmotor' and worked by the picturesque looking 2-4-2 side tanks. The L&Y used rail level entrances to the push and pull units, similar to Great Eastern and Great Western practices. The L&Y and LNWR amalgamated prior to grouping in 1923, the L&Y always being a favourite with enthusiasts.

9. This photograph of Middleton was taken before the grouping and shows the terminus of one of the Lancashire and Yorkshire's shortest branches. The Golden Age of Railways it may have been, with all the private colliery wagons in the yard, but the camera does not lie when one looks for dirt and pollution in the coal burning age. The trackwork is certainly primitive by BR standards, ballast being negligible and the rails well worn. Under LMS ownership the buildings deteriorated and under BR management the roof was demolished. The branch closed to passengers on 7 September, 1964 and to all traffic on 11 October, 1965.

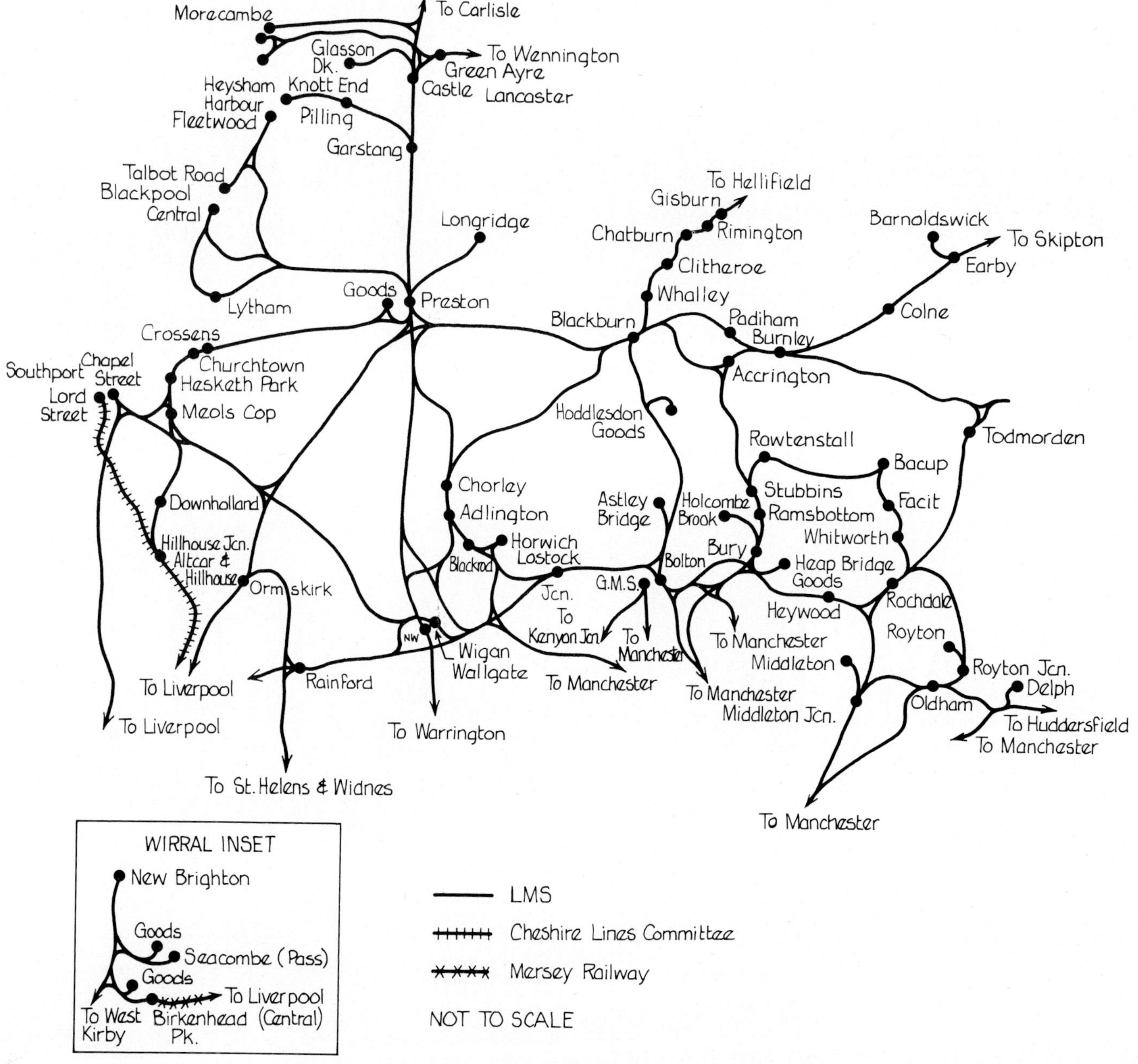

10. Knott End, the deserted terminus of the one time Garstang and Knott End Railway, a small independent concern, in May 1955. The Knott End Railway was independent until the grouping in 1923 when it became part of the LMS system. The passenger service was withdrawn by the LMS on 31 March, 1930, but goods traffic lingered on until 13 November, 1950, when the line was cut back to Pilling. The section from Garstang to Pilling did not close to freight until 1 July, 1963. In the fifties BR were not so prompt in removing track from closed branch lines as they are nowadays and the track in this picture has only just been lifted, some five years after cessation of services.

11. Another view of Middleton, with a Lancashire & Yorkshire tank in a respectable, clean condition on a wet misty day before the grouping. The goods yard seems to be crammed full of wagons.

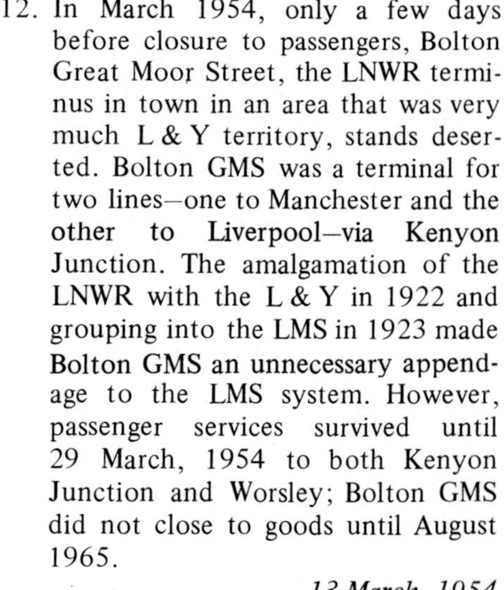

12. In March 1954, only a few days before closure to passengers, Bolton Great Moor Street, the LNWR terminus in town in an area that was very much L & Y territory, stands deserted. Bolton GMS was a terminal for two lines—one to Manchester and the other to Liverpool—via Kenyon Junction. The amalgamation of the LNWR with the L & Y in 1922 and grouping into the LMS in 1923 made Bolton GMS an unnecessary appendage to the LMS system. However, passenger services survived until 29 March, 1954 to both Kenyon Junction and Worsley; Bolton GMS did not close to goods until August 1965.

13 March, 1954

13. Ex-Lancashire & Yorkshire 0-6-0 No 52523 stands at Heap Bridge goods after working tender first down the branch, which closed in December 1973.

28 July, 1962

14. 'Crab' 2-6-0 No 42844 stands at Padiham, the loop from Burnley to Blackburn (which closed to all traffic on 2 November, 1964) having closed on 2 December, 1957 to regular passenger traffic. The loop line was used until the summer of 1963 by Saturday trains, including an oddity which went from Blackpool to Cleethorpes via this route. Note the LMS nameboard.

22 September, 1962

15. Taken at the turn of the century, this view of Glasson Dock shows the impeccable condition of the station buildings, LNWR locomotive and double sided signal arm. The branch closed to passengers on 7 July, 1938 and to freight on 5 October, 1964.

16. Ex-LMS 0-4-4T No 41904 shunting empty stock at Heysham Harbour in April 1952. This port has suffered a decline in importance, having lost the passenger service on 6 October, 1975, following the withdrawal of the shipping service. The ex-LNWR station at Morecambe (Euston Road) closed on 7 September, 1963, having been used for summer only trains since 15 September, 1958 and the nearby Glasson Dock branch closed to freight on 5 October, 1964 and to passengers on 7 July, 1930. The former Midland 'main line' from Heysham to Wennington closed on 5 June, 1967 to all traffic from Lancaster, trains being diverted via Carnforth over the former Furness & Midland Joint line, an example of 'rationalisation'. Passenger services were withdrawn on 3 January, 1966.

17. Longridge, the terminus of the Preston & Longridge Joint line (L & YR and LNWR), seeing plenty of activity as an LNWR 'Super D' 0-8-0 chugs out with a special for Preston. The passenger services were withdrawn on 2 June, 1930 and freight on 16 October, 1967. These venerable old 0-8-0 freight engines could still be seen at work on the London Midland Region as late as the 1960s.

22 September, 1962

18. Former Lancashire & Yorkshire 0-6-0 saddle tank No 51408 stands at Astley Bridge, the terminus of a short goods only branch near Bolton. Opened on 15 October, 1877, this branch had a passenger service for only the first two years of its existence. This ceased on 1 October, 1879 but freight traffic continued for 83 years until 4 September, 1961 from Halliwell to Astley Bridge. The nearby Hoddlesden goods branch closed on 30 October, 1950.

19. A Blackburn train pauses at Churchtown on 23 August, 1961. The Southport to Preston passenger services ceased on 7 September, 1964, as did all traffic from Hesketh Park to Preston. Note the conductor rail; electric services ran from Southport to Crossens, an electrification scheme pioneered by the L & YR as early as 1904. The L & YR ran through from Meols Cop to Altcar on the CLC, but this line was closed on 26 September, 1938 to Downholland, having closed on 15 November, 1926 from Downholland to Hillhouse Junction. Freight over the entire section ceased on 21 January, 1952.

20. A wintry scene at Bacup in December 1966, with a multiple unit train waiting for departure to Manchester. This branch terminus lost its passenger service the following day to Rawtenstall, the service to Rochdale having been withdrawn on 16 June, 1947. Freight services from Bacup to Facit ceased on 11 October, 1954 and to Rawtenstall on 5 December, 1966. Services from Facit to Whitworth finished on 12 August, 1963 and from Whitworth to Rochdale on 21 August, 1967 to freight. The former 'main line' Stubbins to Accrington closed on 5 December, 1966 to all traffic.

3 December, 1966

21. Another famous short L & Y branch which originally had a steam railmotor service was that to Horwich. BR Standard Class 2 2-6-2T No 84013 is seen here about to depart with the 08.10 to Blackrod. Passenger services were withdrawn on 27 September, 1965; the line is still open to serve the BR Works.

17 June, 1961

22. A fine example of Lancashire & Yorkshire architecture can be seen in the station roofing, signal boxes and bracket signals at Middleton Junction, although the tubular posts are standard BR. The lines for Leeds are at the left and those to Oldham to the right; the Middleton bay is round the back of the island.

23. Fleetwood, once upon a time a busy passenger terminal with boat connections for Ireland. Passenger services were withdrawn to Wyre Dock on 18 April, 1966 and from Wyre Dock to Poulton on 1 June, 1970. Freight services still operate to the dock.

7 May, 1955

24. On 28 July, 1962 the Hellifield train is about to leave
Blackburn behind 2-6-4T
No 42484. Blackburn to Hellifield still sees plenty of passenger traffic, usually diversions
on Sundays owing to engineers'
works. Regular passenger services ceased on 10 September,
1962, although the line now
sees ramblers' excursions on
Sundays inaugurated in summer
1978.

25. The other end of the branch
with the 17.10 from Hellifield
to Blackburn about to depart
behind a Class 4F 0-6-0 in a
somewhat filthy condition.

28 May, 1960

26 Blackburn, in 1968, looking completely untouched by the passage of time. This picture could have been taken before the grouping. Each train departure has a clock indicator and fingerboard. Passenger services to Chorley and Wigan were withdrawn on 4 January, 1960, freight to Feniscowles was withdrawn on 22 April, 1968 and from Feniscowles to Chorley on 31 January, 1966. Boars Head to Adlington closed to freight in December 1971. The clock indicates the next train to Colne, now the terminus of the once through line to Skipton. Colne to Skipton closed to all traffic on 2 February, 1970.

18 May, 1968

27. Former L & Y 2-4-2T No 50623 still in LMS livery about to leave Barnoldswick for Earby. The layout at this former Midland terminus was such that in order to run round the train, the gates across the road had to be closed, much to the fury of local motorists. Passenger services on this line ceased on 27 September, 1965 and freight on 1 August, 1966. Barnoldswick was in Yorkshire when this photograph was taken but the town has now been 'moved' into Lancashire.

8 July, 1949

28. Clitheroe, an intermediate station on the Blackburn to Hellifield line in Lancashire and Yorkshire days. Several interesting L & Y features are to be seen here, for instance, the habit of ballasting over the sleepers, the heavy advertising and the huge gas bowls.

29. A Bury to Rochdale train leaves Heywood headed by a Class 4 2-6-4 tank. The passenger service from Rochdale to Bolton was withdrawn on 5 October, 1970 whilst the line from Bury to Bolton closed to all traffic on the same day.

GENTLEMEN
NATIONAL
PEARS

WAY OUT
PASSENGERS MUST NOT
CROSS THE LINE EXCEPT
BY THE SUBWAY
LLEY
PEARS
WAY OUT
PASSENGERS MUST NOT
CROSS THE LINE EXCEPT
BY THE SUBWAY

30 and 31. Two pictures of the Blackburn to Hellifield branch in pre-grouping days; Gisburn (*top*) has spotlessly clean platforms, L & Y signals and concrete flowerpots to hold the shrubs on the nearside platform. Whalley (*below*) shows the L & Y paintwork on the valancing on the roof, which has clear glass to it (most roofs were painted over in the first war) and the Victorian/Edwardian craze for advertising on the fencing. A few well known favourites 'Pears Soap', and 'Wrights Coal Tar Soap' can be seen; these enamel notices were to be found all over Britain.

32. A two car DMU stands at Royton, another short L & Y branch. The passenger and freight service was withdrawn on 18 April, 1966.

3 May, 1963

33. The push-and-pull set headed by L & Y 2-4-2T No 50655 is about to leave Holcombe Brook with the 17.24 to Bury. The branch had a curious history tractionwise. The L & Y electrification schemes in the Liverpool area having been a success, the electric services were extended from Bury to Holcombe Brook on 29 July, 1913. The current was 3,500 volts overhead, but this was replaced by a third rail on 29 March, 1918. The third rail electrification lasted until 24 March, 1951 when it was replaced by steam operation—L & Y 2-4-2 tanks no less! The line closed to passengers on 5 May, 1952 and the train is seen here the previous day with the conductor rails still in position. Freight services from Tottington lasted until 2 May, 1960, and from Bury to Tottington until 19 August, 1963. The L & Y used railmotors with steps that were lowered—a practice similar to that of the Great Western.

4 May, 1952

34. A suburban branch ran to Seacombe on the former Wirral Railway, a small local concern which passed into LMS ownership in 1923. In this picture the Class 3 2-6-2T is still in LMS livery, although with BR number 40080. The branch closed to passengers on 4 January, 1960 and to freight on 17 June, 1963. The nearby New Brighton branch still flourishes with a frequent electric service throughout the day to Liverpool.

17 November, 1951

35. A short LNWR branch worked by push-and-pull trains ran to Delph. In this picture stock is used with drop down steps. 'The Delph Donkey', as the train was known, commenced operations on 1 September, 1851 and ceased on 2 May, 1955. Freight traffic ceased on 4 November, 1963.

36. In 1951 a Class 2 2-6-2T is seen at Rainford Junction with an Ormskirk train. This cross country branch of the former L & Y was closed to passengers on 5 November, 1956, whilst the LNWR branch to St Helens closed to passengers on 18 June, 1951 and to freight on 6 July, 1964. The Ormskirk to Rainford branch closed to freight to Skelmersdale on 18 November, 1963, to White Moss on 4 November, 1963 and to Rainford Junction on 16 September, 1961. Passenger services from St Helens to Widnes were withdrawn on 18 June, 1951.

Yorkshire

The LMS served West Yorkshire and the Pennine branches, some of which ventured to windswept and remote parts of the country. The area was the preserve of the Midland, LNWR and L&Y railways. The Midland built the main line from Settle to Carlisle and the Hawes branch was one of the wildest areas to visit in the winter. The Midland and the LNWR rivalled the North Eastern in the West Riding creating duplicate routes between several large towns. One Midland branch line has been perfectly preserved as the Keighley & Worth Valley Railway.

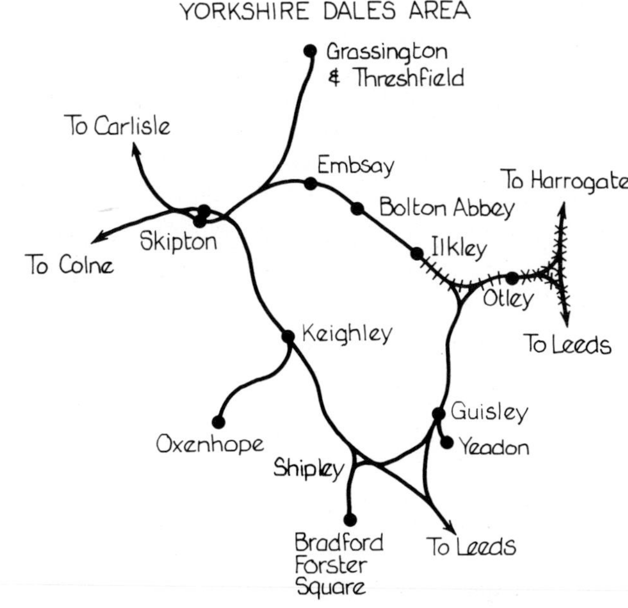

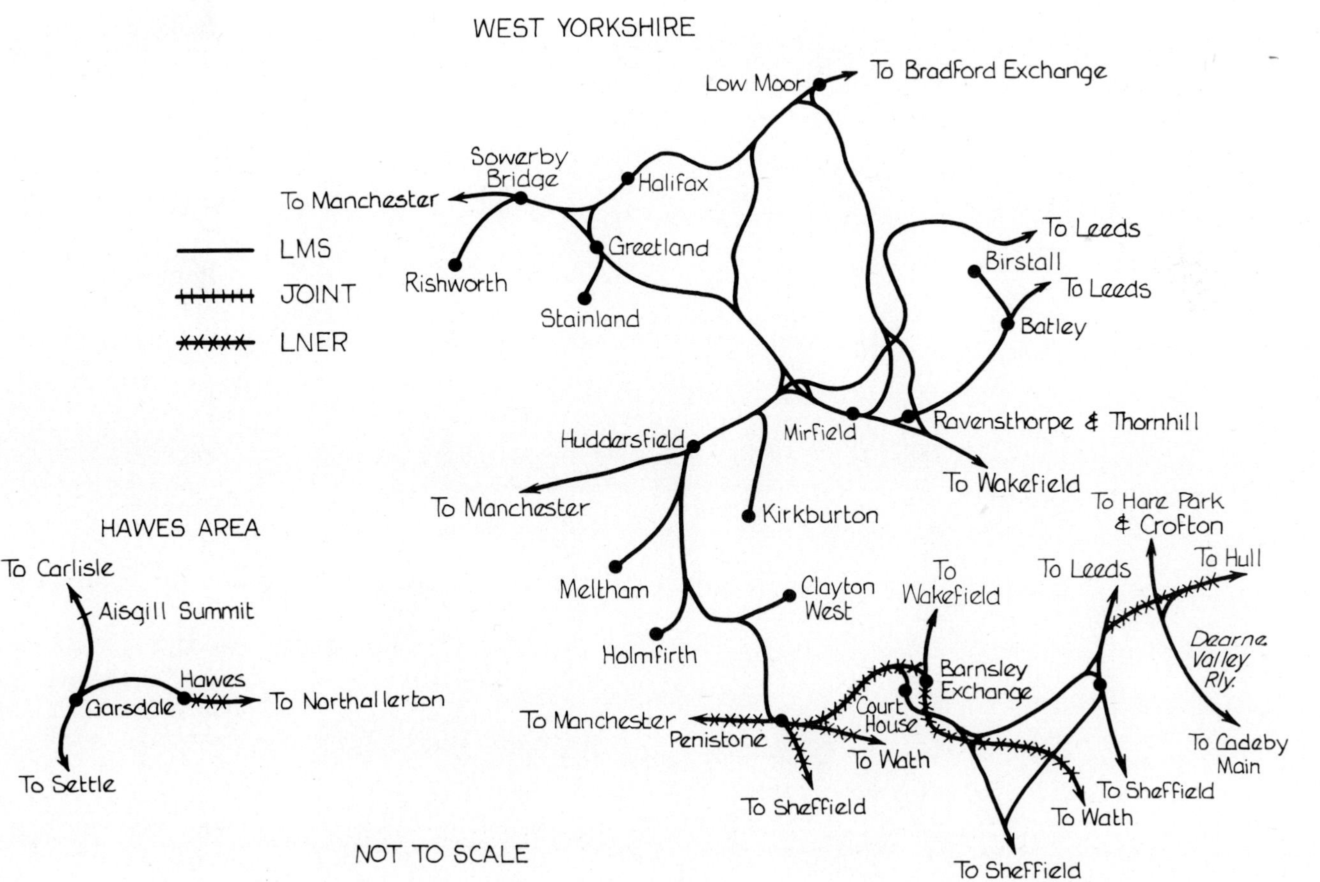

37. Holmfirth, the terminus of a Pennine branch line of the former Lancashire & Yorkshire Railway; a Class 4 2-6-4T waits behind some L & Y stock. The passenger service ceased on 2 November, 1959 and freight on 3 May, 1965. The nearby branch from Huddersfield to Meltham closed to passengers on 23 May, 1949 and to freight on 5 April, 1965.

38. Clayton West in October 1965; the district auditors have pounced and are about to grill the station staff at this small Pennine terminus, which is still open to passengers. The two neighbouring branch lines closed many years ago, all part of the former Huddersfield & Sheffield Junction Railway, a constituent of the Lancashire and Yorkshire.

39. An SLS railtour has arrived at Rishworth, another short L & Y branch line near Halifax. The Rishworth branch closed to passengers on 8 July, 1929 and to freight on 12 February, 1953. Like the Stainland branch (closed to passengers 23 September, 1929 and completely on 14 September, 1959), traffic was killed off by more efficient local bus operation.

40. A familiar enough sight nowadays, the Oxenhope branch train in the bay at Keighley but with a Midland 0-4-4T No 58040. The Oxenhope branch of the former Midland Railway closed on 1 January, 1962, but re-opened on 29 June, 1968 as the Keighley & Worth Valley Railway and has proved to be one of the most successful of the steam worked preserved lines.

41. The Midland Railway ran a few trains a day from Garsdale, formerly Hawes Junction, to Hawes, seen here, the terminus of the North Eastern Railway's Wensleydale line from Northallerton. The branch closed to all traffic on 16 March, 1959, a few days after this photograph was taken.

42. A Class 4 2-6-4T waits at Barnsley Court House with a train to Sheffield via the Midland route. The service was withdrawn from Barnsley to Cudworth on 9 June, 1958, and the station closed and services diverted to Exchange Station in 1960 via a new spur opened in that year. Two other short branch lines in the South Yorkshire area were to Dewsbury Market Place (L & YR), closed to passengers on 1 December, 1930 and to freight on 6 February, 1961, and the Dewsbury Savile Town branch (Midland), closed on 18 December, 1950. The Sheffield and Rotherham original terminus at Rotherham Westgate was in use until 6 October, 1952 when the line closed to all traffic.

14 May, 1951

43. A view of the terminus at Over & Wharton in 1950. This short branch closed as a wartime economy measure on 1 January, 1917 but reopened on 12 July, 1920. Passenger services were finally withdrawn by the LMS on 16 June, 1947.

44. The Dearne Valley train runs up to Cadeby Main signal box to run Class 2 2-6-2T No 41284 round its train and the crew pose with the signalman. The Dearne Valley Railway was promoted by local coal owners to enable better outlets for the shipment of their coal. The Dearne Valley allied itself to the Hull & Barnsley to start with but then changed sides and became worked by the Lancashire & Yorkshire and therefore the LMS. The L & Y introduced a steam railmotor service in 1912 and the passenger service lasted until 10 September, 1951. The Dearne Valley was closed to freight on 11 July, 1966, except the collieries that were served by a new spur from the Midland main line at Houghton which runs to Bamburgh and Goldthorpe.

7 April, 1951

45 and 46. On a Sunday in 1961 Class 4F 0-6-0 No 44220 has arrived at Grassington & Threshfield, to give the station its full name, with a ramblers' excursion from Skipton. Midland features here are the Midland Railway signal box in North Eastern Region colours (blue and white), the Midland signals and a trespass notice conveniently situated in the garden of an adjacent pub! The Grassington branch closed to passengers on 22 September, 1930, but Sunday excursions ran until the 1960s. The Midland also ran from Skipton to Ilkley which closed to passengers on 22 March, 1965 and on 5 July, 1965 to freight. The freight service from Grassington to Rylstone ceased on 11 August, 1969. Another curious branch line in the area was that from Guiseley to Yeadon which had a passenger service only occasionally, in the form of excursions. The branch was traversed by railtours in 1953 and closed to freight on 10 August, 1964.

47. Heaths Junction, Biddulph in the spring of 1953 with ex-LMS Class 4F 0-6-0 No 44500 heading a traditional British unbraked freight train clanking along with china clay and coal in wagons of various sizes. The signalling is also pre-grouping. The Biddulph Valley line from Congleton to Bucknall closed to passengers on 11 July, 1927, the service from Bucknall to Stoke being withdrawn on 7 May, 1956. Heaths Junction to Congleton, Brunswick Wharf closed on 1 April, 1968 and Heaths Junction to Ford Green in April 1976, both to all traffic.

48. Hulme End looking towards the buffer stops of this 2 ft 6 in gauge line in 1931. Although closed in 1934 a picture of the most famous of all the LMS branch lines deserves a showing if only for the comparison with present day Indian narrow gauge lines, for which the rolling stock had a great similarity.

Cheshire, Shropshire and Staffordshire

The North Stafford Railway, centred on Stoke-on-Trent, was entirely a local railway, although it posssessed wide running powers and North Stafford trains turned up in all sorts of places. The Knotty—as the NSR was known locally—was held in high esteem by the local people and even today is referred to with a certain reverence. The North Stafford had a narrow gauge line which the LMS inherited at grouping. The Leek & Manifold Railway, built on the 2 ft 6 in gauge and opened on 27 June, 1904, was closed by the LMS on 12 March, 1934. The course of this line which would now-adays be a wonderful tourist attraction, can still be walked, as the LMS donated the trackbed to Staffordshire County Council in 1937. The Waterhouses to Leek branch, which connected with the narrow gauge Leek and Manifold line, closed to passengers on 30 September, 1935 and freight services ceased from Caldon Junction to Waterhouses on 1 March, 1943. The Caldon Low branch remains open for freight traffic. Another line in Cheshire, that from Chester to Whitchurch closed to passenger traffic on 19 September, 1957 and to all traffic on 23 March, 1964. Passenger services from Leek Brook North Junction to Stoke Junction were withdrawn on 7 May, 1966.

◁ 49. Oakamoor, on the Churnet Valley line which is still open from Stoke-on-Trent, but the section from Leek to North Rode closed to passengers on 7 November, 1960 and completely on 15 June, 1964. Leek Brook Junction to Leek closed completely on 6 July, 1970 and the section from Oakamoor to Uttoxeter closed to all traffic on 4 January, 1965. Passenger services over the section from Leek to Uttoxeter were withdrawn on 4 January, 1965. The nearby branch to Ashbourne closed to all traffic from Rocester on 1 June, 1964, the passenger service having been withdrawn on 1 November, 1954.

11 September, 1954

◁ 50. A Market Drayton train hauled by Class 4 2-6-4T No 42323 stands at Keele; note the standard LMS nameboard, cast iron mounted in a wooden frame in this instance painted over in the LMR colours. LMS nameboard and notices were yellow and black, similar to the Great Northern of Ireland. The branch from Market Drayton to Stoke-on-Trent closed to passengers from Market Drayton to Silverdale on 7 May, 1956 and from Silverdale to Stoke-on-Trent on 2 March, 1964. The freight traffic ceased on 14 February, 1966, from Madeley. A spur was constructed called 'the Madeley Chord', from the West Coast Line to Silverdale. Alsager Road to Keele closed to passengers on 27 April, 1931 and to freight on 7 January, 1963.

11 September, 1954

51. Cheadle, in the summer of 1960 with a LMS Class 4 2-6-4T running round the train from Cresswell. The branch was realigned by the LMS in 1933. When the tunnel needed renewal the LMS simply built a new line around it. The Cheadle branch closed on 17 June, 1963.

52. An early morning Ditton Junction to Broadheath train hauled by a Class 2 2-6-2T has stopped for water from an ancient LNWR column at Warrington Low Level. The signals are also LNWR lower quadrants. The line closed to passengers on 10 September, 1962.

53. Shortly after closure, Stirchley, on the LNWR Coalport branch, is slowly being engulfed by weeds and wild flowers.

54. The compact station buildings at Coalport on the short LNWR branch from Wellington, which was also the terminus of the cross country Stafford to Wellington line, which closed to passengers on 7 September, 1964. Stafford to Newport closed on 1 August, 1966 and to Donnington on 1 July, 1968, to freight. The Coalport branch closed to passengers on 2 June, 1952 and to freight on 5 December, 1960.

Clwyd and Gwynedd

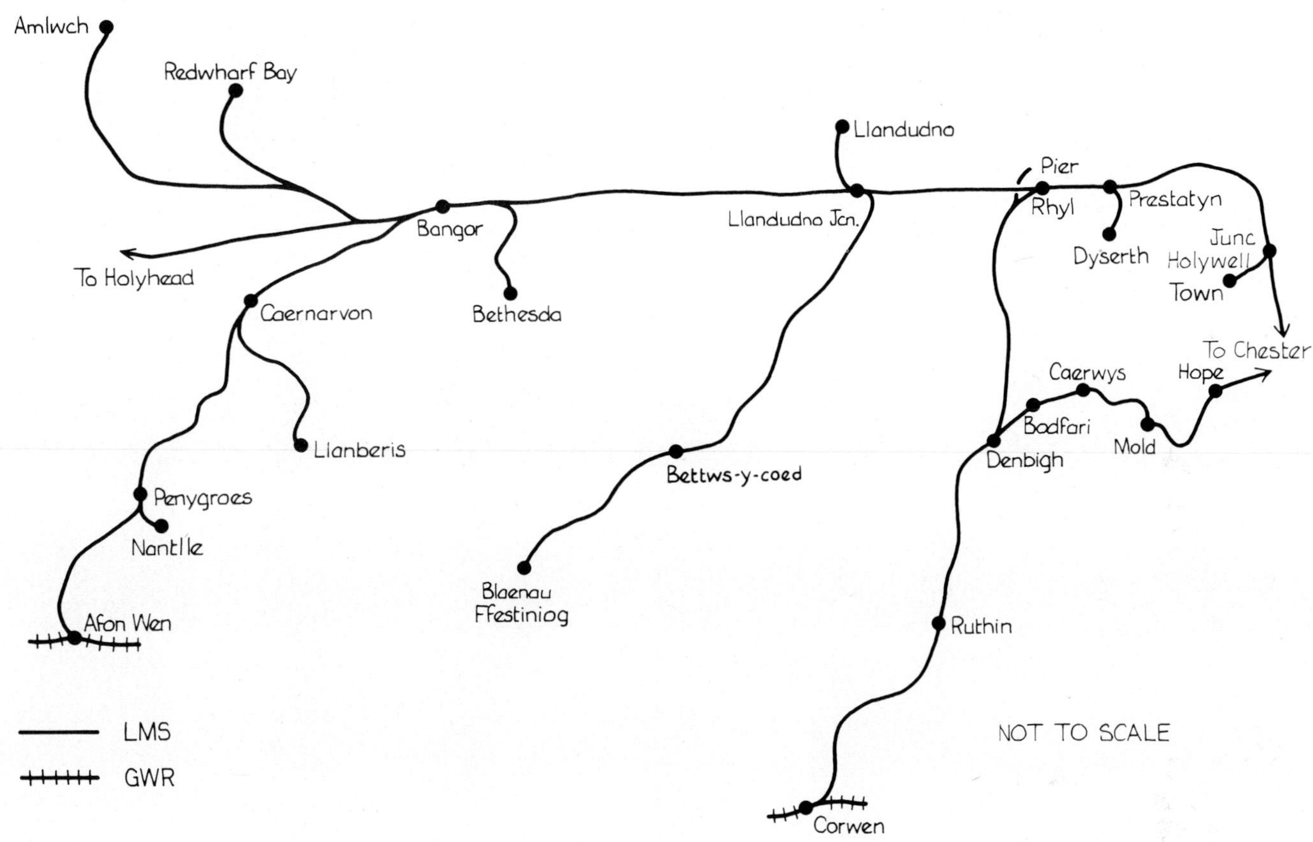

The LNWR main line from Chester to Holyhead was fed by branch lines throughout its length, most of which originated in small Welsh towns and traversed some splendid countryside, often with mountainous backgrounds. The 'Cambrian Radio Cruise' train traversed the North Wales branch lines until their closure. The train was a mixture of ancient saloons of Midland, LNWR and LMS stock fitted with comfortable furniture and the passengers were treated to a running commentary as the train passed through to magnificent North Wales scenery. The closure of the Rhyl to Corwen line in 1962 finished this marvellous train off. With the completion of the Ffestiniog Railway to Blaenau Ffestiniog in the near future, a through route will be established once again between the coast and the mountain areas inland.

55. Autumn mists descend on the former LNWR station at
Amlwch at which is standing a multiple unit set from
Bangor. The station had a home made nameboard
made out of old rope nailed on to a wooden board,
seen behind the flowerbeds to the right of the train.
The line closed to passengers on 7 December, 1964.

56. Red Wharf Bay, the former LNWR passenger station
still in LMS paint, a few years after closure to all
traffic on 3 April, 1950; passenger services were withdrawn on 22 September, 1930.

57 and 58..
Caernarvon (*top*), with MLS/SLS special to Afon Wen in 1963 headed by two Ivatt Class 2 2-6-2 tanks with, strangely enough, an express passenger headcode! The lower picture shows Afon Wen with the Great Western lower quadrants on wooden posts. The Class 4 2-6-4 tank (on the right) has the right of way over the 'North Wales Land Cruise', (seen on the left), headed by a Class 2 2-6-2T and the unusual collection of stock that formed that train. The leading vehicle is an LNWR first in BR cream and red livery. The Afon Wen to Caernarvon line closed to all traffic on 7 December, 1964.

59. A study of LNWR architecture at Mold on the Chester to Denbigh branch, closed to passengers on 30 April, 1962. Freight services on the line were withdrawn from Denbigh to Rhydymyn on the same date, from Rhydymyn to Mold on 1 January, 1968 and Chester to Hope Junction on 2 February, 1970.

60. Hope & Penyffordd, on the Chester to Denbigh line with a few passengers waiting for the train. The LNWR nameboard and station signs with raised lettering have been painted over in BR maroon with white letters. The LNWR oil lamps on wooden posts are predominant here as are the LNWR sheds for storage of goods.

61 and 62. In the upper picture a Class 4 2-6-4T stands at Ruthin on the Chester train whilst a Class 4F
0-6-0 in the goods yard completes this LMS scene. The station valancing is very decorative, as are the
ventilators on the 'gents' roof behind the gas lighting. The 'Vale of Clwyd' as the line was known ran
from Rhyl to Corwen but the line closed to passengers in sections: from Rhyl to Denbigh on
19 September, 1955, Denbigh to Ruthin on 30 April, 1962 and Ruthin to Corwen on 2 February, 1953.
The lower picture shows the same train at Denbigh with ornate gothic station buildings behind the train
in April 1962. Freight services were withdrawn from Corwen to Ruthin on 30 April, 1962, from Ruthin
to Denbigh on 1 March, 1965 and from Denbigh to Rhyl on 1 January, 1968.

65 and 66. Scenes in October 1963 as a special heads for Llanberis from Bangor. The engine shed at Bangor (right) is still full of LMR types. The picture below shows the train at Llanberis standing at a LNWR signal. Passenger services to Llanberis were withdrawn on 12 September, 1932, but excursions ran until September 1962. Freight finished on 7 September, 1964.

63. Class 3 2-6-2T No 40208 has just arrived at Bettws-y-Coed, with the 12.25 Llandudno Junction to Blaenau Ffestiniog. Note the pre-grouping coach in the sidings, probably ex Midland.

8 September, 1952

64. Blaenau Ffestiniog, with the former LNWR terminus on the right and the Ffestiniog station on the left behind the LNWR building. The Llandudno Junction branch is still open and Blaenau Ffestiniog will form an interchange between the Ffestiniog and the BR line. The new station on the site of the former GWR station, will be joint British Rail and Ffestiniog Railway.

3 July, 1950

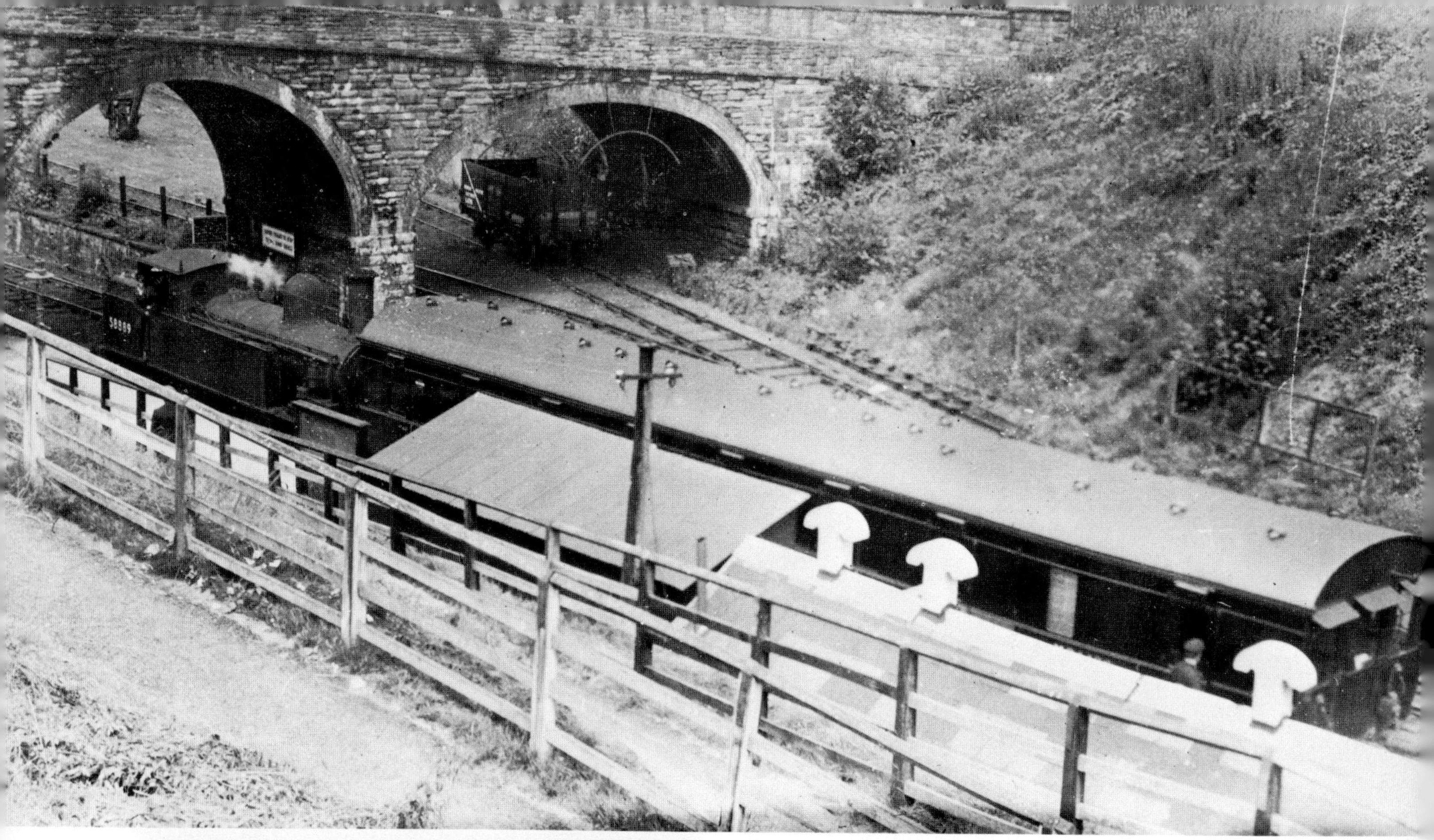

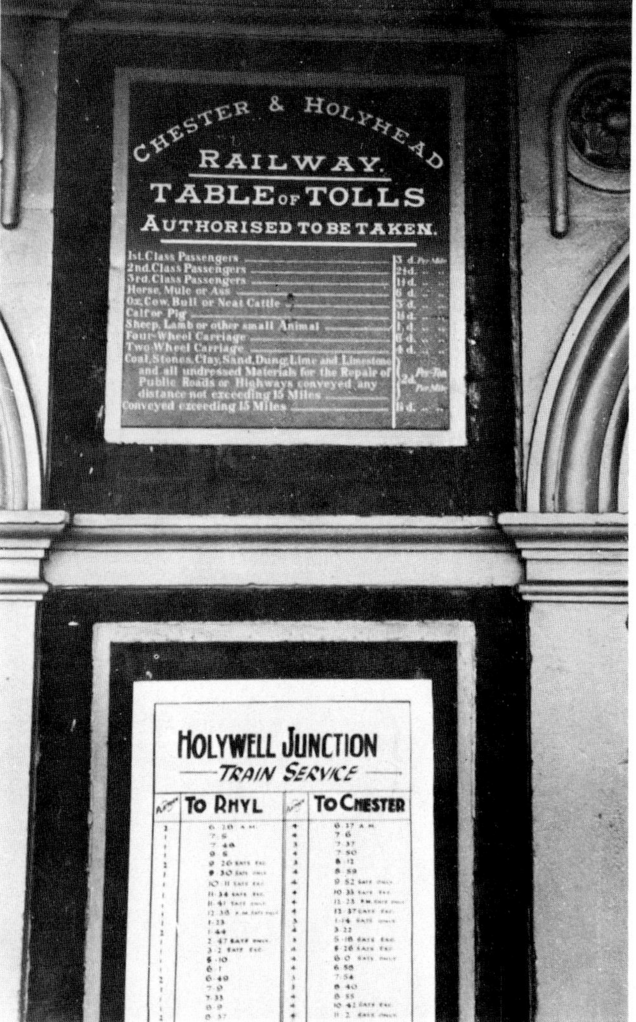

67 and 68. The push-and-pull train rests at Holywell on 5 July, 1949, worked by Webb 0-6-2 'Coal Tank' No 58889. (*Below*) The fare table at Holywell Junction still displaying the Chester & Holyhead Railway fares. The branch closed to all traffic on 6 September, 1954.

69 and 70. (*Above*) The station buildings at Nantlle, ▷ seen in 1963 have been long disused as the branch closed to passengers on 8 August, 1932, freight finishing 31 years later on 2 November, 1963 shortly after this photograph was taken. (*Below*) The branch as seen at the approach to the terminus with an SLS special and mountains in the background in October 1963.

71 and 72.
(*Above*) A passenger special at Bethesda, in fact probably the last train as the line closed to all traffic on 7 October, 1963, having closed to regular passenger trains on 3 December, 1951. (*Centre*) The once spacious station buildings at Bethesda.

73.
Another similar branch in the locality—the branch to Dyserth, off the Chester & Holyhead main line—closed to passengers on 22 September, 1930. It must have been one of the smallest stations in Britain.

Derbyshire and Nottinghamshire

The Peak area was served by the Midland and LNWR. The area also contained the unusual goods only Cromford & High Peak Railway with the 1 in 14 Hopton incline worked by North London Railway tanks, and the Nottingham coalfield where some of the branch lines closed as early as 1926.

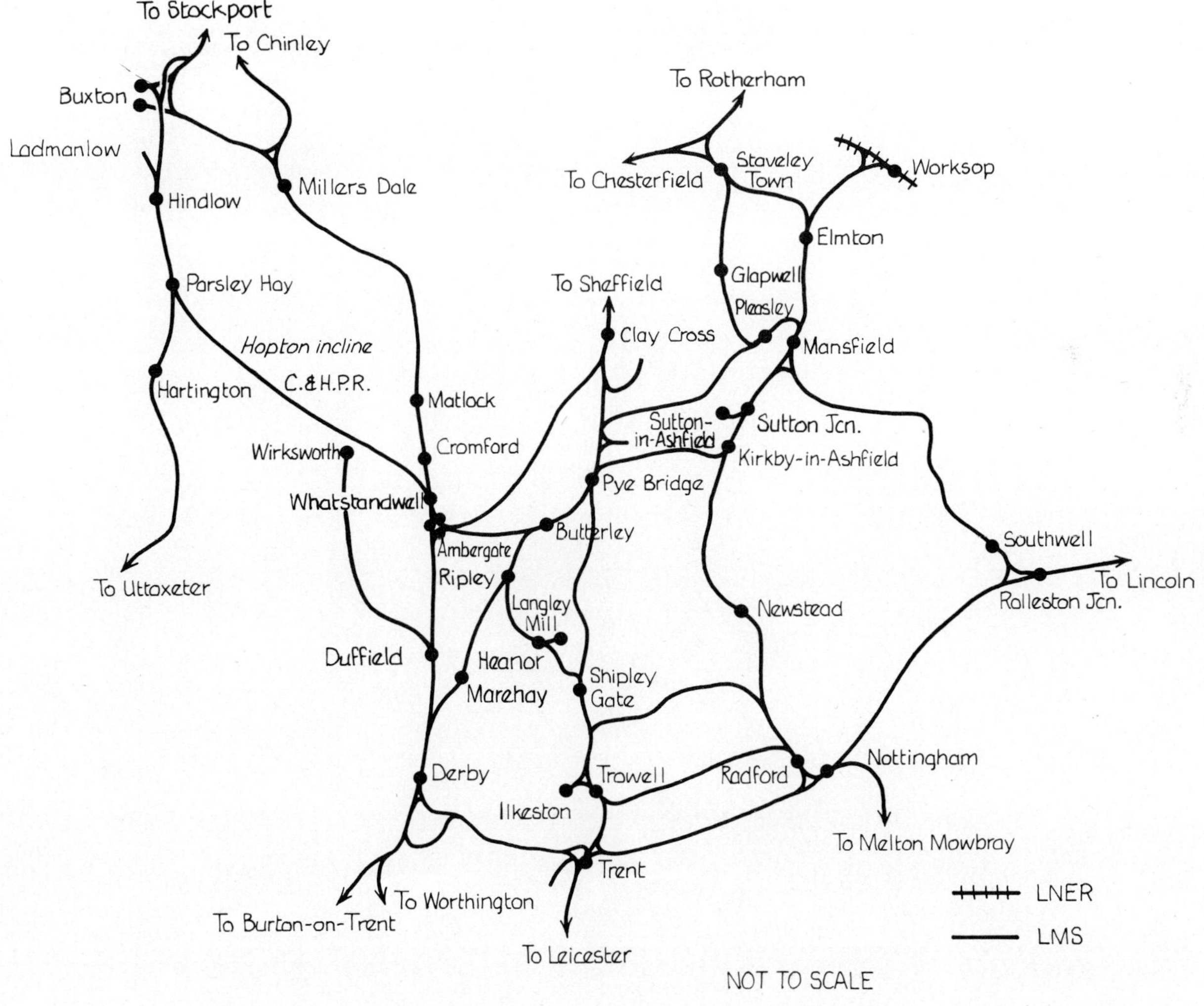

◁ 74. A Miller's Dale train reposes at Buxton headed by an LMS 0-4-4T No 41905, design of 1932, built as a post grouping version of the Midland 0-4-4, a rare class of 10 engines. Buxton to Miller's Dale closed to passenger traffic on 6 March, 1967.

75. Fowler Class 4 2-6-4T No 42315 heads a Manchester to Buxton passenger train out of Middlewood. The LNWR line to Buxton is still open for passenger traffic, but the LNWR line on to Ashbourne closed to passengers on 1 November, 1954, and to freight to Hartington on 7 October, 1963 and to Briggs Sidings on 2 October, 1967.

76. On 13 March, 1925 a trial run of an experimental Sentinel railcar has arrived at Ripley. Two Sentinel railcars were sold to the Jersey Eastern Railway. The LMS eventually bought 14 Sentinel railcars from the makers but they proved to be unsuccessful and were not ordered on a large scale.

The passenger service to Derby and Butterley was withdrawn on 1 June, 1930, the service from Ripley to Langley Mill having been withdrawn on 4 May, 1926 as a result of the General Strike. The section from Ripley to Marehay closed to freight on 1 April, 1963 and to Denby North on 29 July, 1968. The Heanor branch closed to goods traffic on 1 September, 1951.

77 and 78. Scenes on the Mansfield line; Newstead (*above*), with Class 4 2-6-4 No 42221 on the 12.25 Nottingham to Worksop (*Below*) Kirkby-in-Ashfield on 2 May, 1964, from which the passenger service was withdrawn on 12 October, 1964. The service from Mansfield to Staveley Town via Pleasley was withdrawn on 28 July, 1930. The connecting line from Elmton to Chesterfield closed to passengers on 5 July, 1954, although summer Saturday trains ran until August 1962. The short Sutton-in-Ashfield branch closed on 1 October, 1951 and Ilkeston Town on 22 August, 1964 both to all traffic, the latter having closed to passengers on 16 June, 1947.

79 and 80. Scenes on the Southwell branch. (*Above*) The Midland scene at Southwell in 1895 complete with home signal and black dot. (*Below*) The guard checks his watch as Midland 0-4-4T No 1324 waits for the 'right away' on 12 April, 1952. Southwell to Rolleston Junction closed to passengers on 15 June, 1959, whilst the service to Mansfield was withdrawn on 12 August, 1929. Freight services from Rolleston Junction closed to passengers on 15 June, 1959, whilst the service to Blidworth to Southwell on 1 March, 1965.

81.
Rolleston Junction, with a view of the pre-grouping branch train. A Midland 0-4-4 tank and LNWR coach (push and pull fitted), Midland lamp-posts, fencing and signal box can be seen.

12 April, 1952

82.
The famous Hopton Incline of the Cromford & High Peak Railway, with ex-North London Railway 0-6-0T No 7527 blasting up the 1 in 14 gradient. The line closed on 1 May, 1967, there never having been any passenger service.

83.
Wirksworth, with a visit by the SLS/MLS using Midland 0-4-4 tank No 58077 and LMS open stock in early BR cream and red colours. The line is still open for freight traffic, passenger services having been discontinued on 1 January, 1949.

West Midlands, Warwickshire and Worcestershire

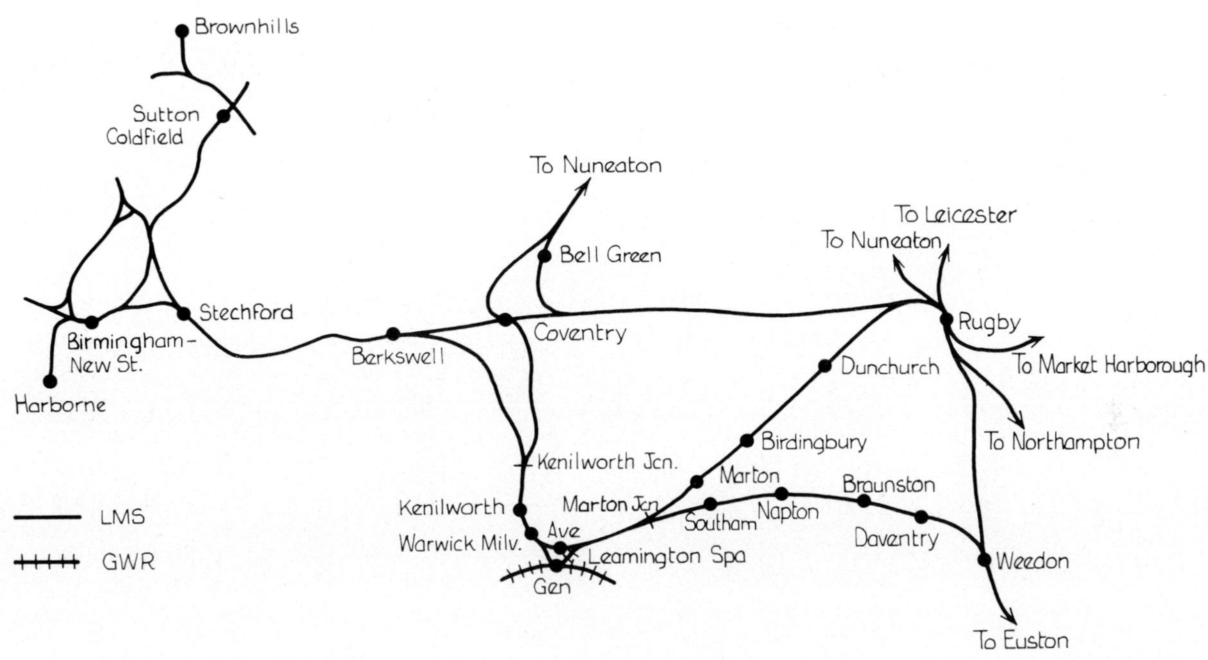

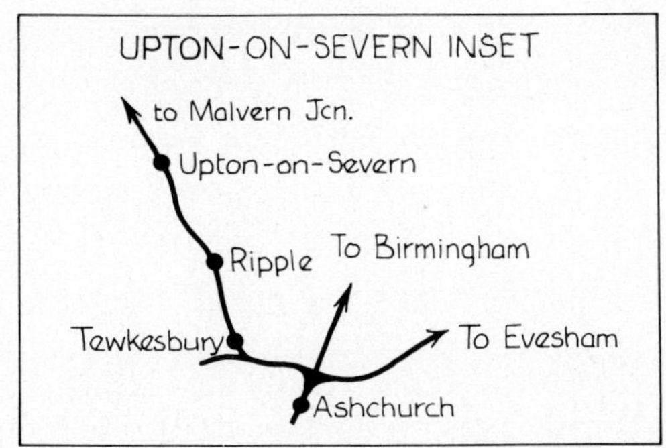

The former Midland Railway and LNWR were great rivals for the traffic of the Black Country in the Birmingham and Wolverhampton area. The LMS as successor to the MR and LNWR had to contend for traffic against the Great Western. Today the Great Western has lost out on the passenger traffic, for the former main route through Birmingham has been closed and Snow Hill now lies derelict, whilst New Street is a modern busy main line station.

84 and 85. Scenes on the Upton-on-Severn branch with (*above*) LMS 0-4-4T
No 41900 of 1932 about to depart on the 13.30 to Ashchurch on 23 August,
1958 and (*below*) Midland Class 3F No 43754 at Ashchurch. The line
to Upton-on-Severn went through to Malvern Wells under Midland auspices
and in the other direction from Ashchurch to Barnt Green via Evesham.
The Great Malvern to Upton-on-Severn section of line closed on 1 December,
1952 to all traffic and that from Tewkesbury to Upton-on-Severn on
1 July, 1963 and on to Ashchurch on 2 November, 1964. Passenger services
were withdrawn from Ashchurch to Upton-on-Severn on 14 August, 1961.
The line from Ashchurch to Redditch closed to passengers on 1 October,
1962 and the part from Evesham to Alcester was closed to all traffic on the
same date. Freight services between Ashchurch and Evesham were withdrawn
on 9 September, 1963 and between Alcester and Redditch on 6 July, 1964.

86. Ivatt Class 2 2-6-2T No 41227 pauses ▷
at Birdingbury with a Leamington to
Rugby push-and-pull train, with LMS
nameboard prominent to the left.
The line closed to passengers on
15 June, 1959 and the part from
Leamington to Marton Junction was
closed to all traffic on 4 April, 1966.

87. Leamington Spa Avenue, looking ▷
towards Rugby in 1958. The LMS
station was alongside the present
(GWR) station and little can be seen
of the LMS station today. The LMS
station was the centre for four lines,
the direct line to Coventry being the
only one now in use, although the
passenger service from Coventry to
Nuneaton closed on 18 January,
1965, the same day as the short
Berkswell to Kenilworth line, which
lost its freight services on 17 January,
1969.

88 and 89.
Two views of the Leamington to Weedon branch which closed to passengers on 15 September, 1958 and to freight in two sections: on 2 December, 1963 from Weedon to Napton, and on 5 November, 1962 from Napton to Southam. The Southam to Marton Junction section remains open for cement trains from Rugby. The upper picture shows Southam with the LMS push-and-pull train from Weedon, whilst the lower shows Braunston Station with the push-and-pull propelled by Class 2 tank No 41285.

90. The Leamington to Rugby
push-and-pull propelled by
Class 2 tank No 41227 leaves
Dunchurch. The station buildings are still oil lit in this 1959
photograph.

91. Harborne was the terminus of a
Black Country branch line here
seen with an LNWR tank at the
turn of the century. The branch
closed to passengers on
22 November, 1934 and was
popular with railtour organisers.
The line closed to freight
traffic on 4 November, 1963.
Another line in the Birmingham area that closed in the
thirties was the Midland branch
to Brownhills, which closed to
passengers on 31 March, 1930
and in September 1960 to
freight.

92 and 93. Loughborough Derby Road, or the LNWR station in town, in what was very much Midland territory. The top picture shows the passenger terminus falling into disrepair in 1951. The lower picture shows the exterior of the station in 1951. The Loughborough Derby Road branch passenger service to Nuneaton ceased on 13 April, 1931, the same day as the Moira to Shackerstone line. Freight traffic ceased from Loughborough to Shepshed on 30 November, 1955, and from Shepshed to Coalville on 11 December, 1963.

The East Midlands lines of the LMS included the former
Midland and LNWR railways and featured some traditional
branch railways and cross country lines including the former
Stratford-on-Avon and Midland Junction Railway, a line
not blessed with much in the way of passenger traffic but
very useful as a through route from East to West. The Midland found the through line very useful in connecting up
the two parts of the system. The Leicester & Swannington
Railway was one of the oldest in the former Midland
system and it was here that the steam whistle was reputed
to have been invented.

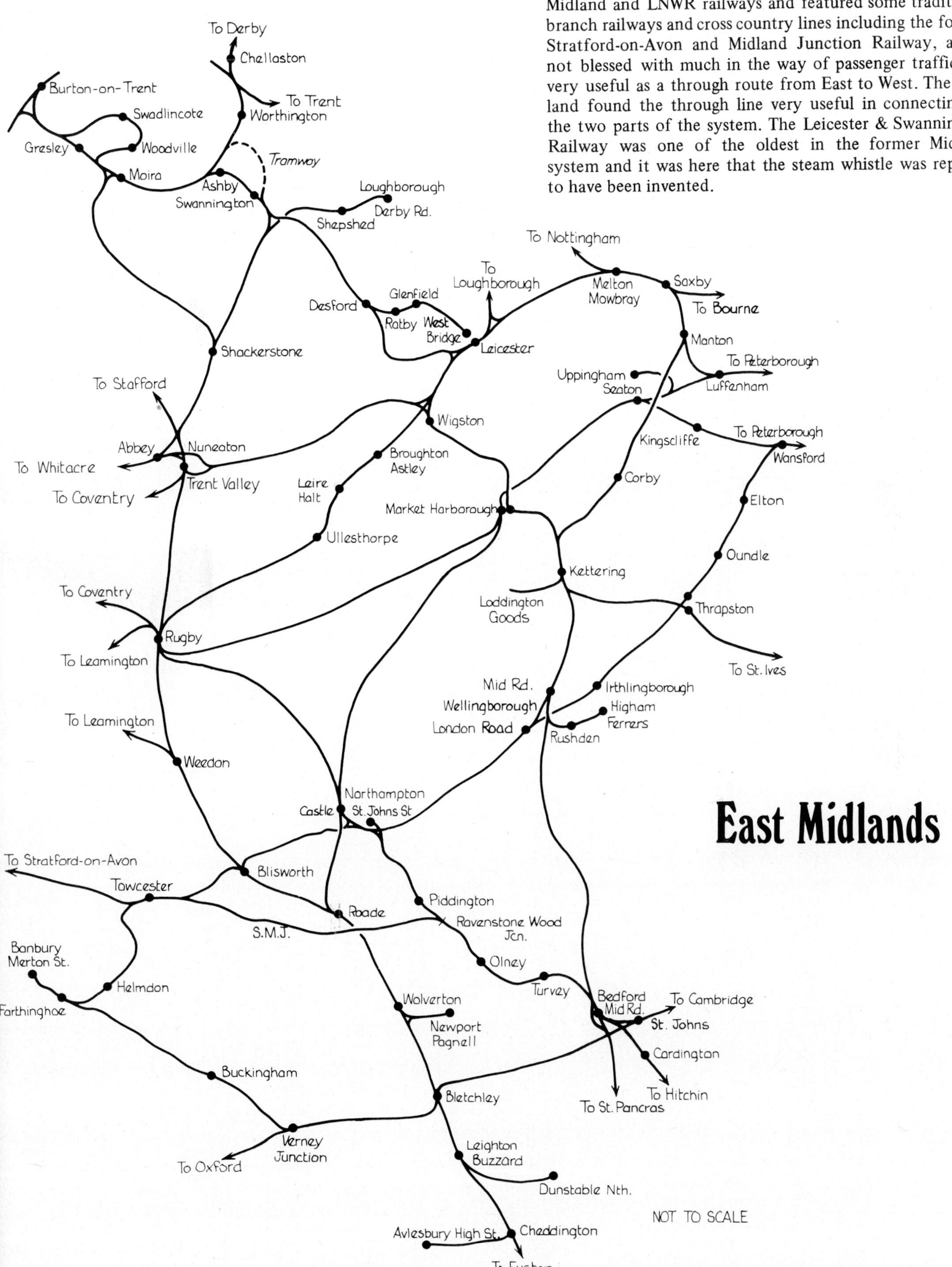

94. Two Midland Class 2F 0-6-0s of nineteenth century vintage chug through Glenfield to Leicester West Bridge with the daily goods.

95. A passenger's view of the station at Swadlincote on the Swadlincote loop line in April 1957. The regular passenger service was withdrawn on 6 October, 1947 but summer Saturday trains ran until September 1962. The branch was used for wagon storage after freight ceased and closed finally to all traffic in the late sixties, in about 1969. Passenger services were withdrawn on the Leicester–Burton line on 7 September, 1964.

96. Glenfield, another view of the small Midland station with the well known tunnel in the background. This station was on the Leicester & Swannington Railway, one of the earliest standard gauge constituents of the Midland. The Leicester & Swannington included two cable worked inclines and a tramway in its operations and was reputed to be where the whistle on locomotives was invented. The line ran through to and connected with the Ashby to Derby line, which closed to passengers on 22 September, 1930 and on 22 January, 1968 from Worthington to Newlount Colliery.

97. The notorious Glenfield tunnel, of horseshoe shape and nearly one mile long. There was no clearance between train and walls and no manhole recesses, so permanent way gangs had to watch out! The line closed to freight on 2 May, 1966, having closed to passengers on 24 September, 1928.

98 and 99. Views of the Leicester to Rugby branch, formerly on the 'main line' from London to Scotland, before the East Coast Route was built. This branch closed to all traffic on 1 January, 1962. The upper view shows Broughton Astley, with Midland lamp-posts, fencing and a Class 3F 0-6-0 arriving on a goods. The lower picture shows Leire Halt, one of the intermediate unstaffed halts.

100.
A view of the staggered platforms at Ulles-
thorpe, a former Midland Railway
country station on the Leicester to
Rugby line, which closed to all traffic
on 1 January, 1962. In the background
is a Midland signal box 'switched out'
with signals left in the 'off' position.

101.
The Stratford-on-Avon & Midland
Junction Railway bay platform at
Blisworth with Class 4F 0-6-0 No 44587
about to depart with the 12.45 Blisworth
to Stratford-on-Avon. In the background
can be seen the West Coast main line, since
modernised and electrified. Blisworth
to Stratford-on-Avon closed to passengers
on 7 April, 1952. The branch to Northampton closed on 4 January, 1960, although used until 3 January, 1966 by
diverted passenger trains. The freight
service to Northampton ceased on
6 January, 1969.

15 September, 1951

102.
A general view of Towcester in 1960 when the former Stratford-on-Avon & Midland Junction Railway was open for freight only, the passenger service having been withdrawn to Stratford-on-Avon on 7 April, 1952. The Stratford to Broom Junction section closed to passengers on 23 May, 1949. The Blisworth line runs off to the left of the box and the Olney line to the right. The passenger service from Olney to Towcester operated by Midland Railway trains, ran from 1 December, 1892 until 30 March, 1893 and the line finally closed, being more of a success for freight traffic, on 30 June, 1958. Blisworth to Woodford West closed **to** freight on 3 February, 1964.

103.
Helmdon, looking towards Towcester in 1958, seven years after closure to passengers on 2 July, 1951 and 29 October, 1951, to freight. The former Northampton & Banbury Junction Railway became the Stratford-upon-Avon & Midland Junction Railway in 1910 and was absorbed into the LMS in 1923. The station garden seems to have been overcome by weeds; although the tracks have gone, the station buildings are still in one piece.

104.
Another 1958 view of Helmdon, a former Northampton & Banbury Junction Railway station, showing how quickly nature takes over when a station becomes abandoned.

105.
A return race special about to leave Towcester for Bedford via Ravenstone Wood Junction headed by two Midland Class 4F 0-6-0s. The freight services from Blisworth to Woodford West ceased on 3 February, 1964, and to Stratford-on-Avon by June 1965, Broom Junction to Stratford having closed on 13 June, 1960. Fenny Compton to Kineton remains in situ—the only part of the system that has not been abandoned.

106.
A short branch line ran to Uppingham in the former county of Rutland owned by the LNWR and closed to passengers on 13 June, 1960. Freight traffic was withdrawn on 1 June, 1964. The branch from Seaton to Luffenham, also worked by Ivatt Class 2 2-6-2Ts, and the Peterborough (East) to Market Harborough line closed to all traffic on 6 June, 1966.

11 October, 1958

108.
'Black Five' No 44682, hauling the 09.46 Peterborough to Northampton, arrives at Wellingborough, London Road. This was not so much a branch line as a cross country route. The station has a magnificent assortment of Victorian platform furniture, seats, barrows and notice boards. Passenger services between Peterborough and Northampton were withdrawn on 4 May, 1964. Freight services over the line were withdrawn piecemeal, Northampton to Wellingborough, London Road on 1 August, 1966, Irthlingborough on 6 June, 1966, Thrapston on 7 June, 1965, Oundle on 4 May, 1964 and Peterborough on 6 November, 1972.

11 April, 1964

109.
Cardington was the first station out on the Bedford to Hitchin branch, once the main line from the Midlands to London, as the Midland had to use this route before St Pancras was built to gain access to the Metropolis. Some very Midland features can be seen here, such as the ornate ironwork in the windows, the use of red brick **as** distinct from the LNWR blue brick, and the Midland slanting fencing, similar to the North Eastern and L & Y. The Bedford to Hitchin branch closed to passengers on 1 January, 1962, freight was discontinued in sections: Bedford to Cardington on 29 April, 1969, Shefford on 28 December, 1964 and Hitchin on 30 December, 1963.

107.
The Uppingham branch was worked by interesting motive power and the locomotive seen here is an ex LT & SR 'Atlantic' tank No 41975, classified by BR as '3P'. Notice the B.T.C. advertisement for York Museum by the station entrance.

24 April, 1959

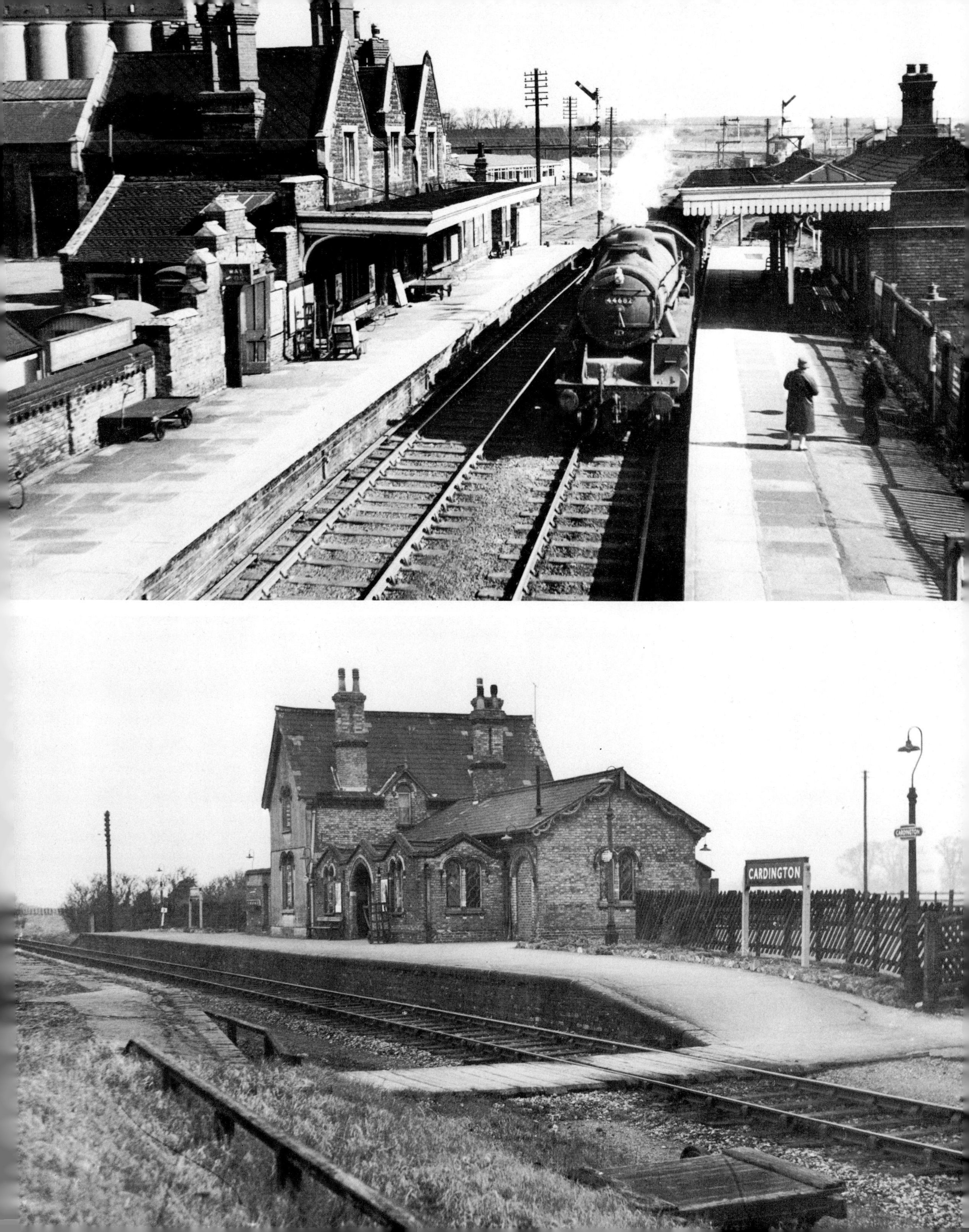

110, 111 and 112.
The declining years of the former LNWR terminus at Aylesbury High Street. The branch opened on 10 June, 1839, connecting at Cheddington with the London & Birmingham Railway and was one of the first branch lines of that system. The exterior (*top*) is seen on 19 July, 1952: the Webb 2-4-2T (*centre*) worked trains on 31 January, 1953, the last day of passenger services. The station was subsequently used for wagon storage (*bottom*), as seen in 1956. The freight services ceased on 12 December, 1963.

113 and 114.

The short Midland branch from Wellingborough was originally intended to continue to Raunds but the promoter's money ran out so the line terminated at Higham Ferrers, BR Standard Class 2 2-6-2T No 84006 has just arrived with a push-and-pull train from Wellingborough (*right*), photographed in 1958. The second view (*below right*) shows the detail in the station buildings and the gas lighting added as an afterthought. The branch closed to passengers on 15 June, 1959 and to freight on 3 November, 1969. Another Midland branch line in the vicinity was the Kettering to St Ives line, also closed to passengers on 15 June, 1959. The line from Huntingdon to Kimbolton closed completely on 15 June, 1959, Kimbolton to Twywell to all traffic on 28 October, 1963 and Twywell to Kettering on 20 March, 1978.

117.
Class 2 2-6-2T No 41275 at Buckingham
with the Buckingham to Verney Junction
push-and-pull. The platforms are very low
necessitating the use of step boards to
get on to the train. The passenger services
from Banbury to Buckingham were withdrawn on 2 January, 1961 and to Verney
Junction on 7 September, 1964. Freight
services ceased on 2 December, 1963 to
Banbury and to Verney Junction on
5 December, 1966.

◁ 115.
Newport Pagnell sees Ivatt Class 2 2-6-2T
No 41222 in 1963. The branch closed to
all traffic on 22 May, 1967, having closed
to passengers on 7 September, 1964.

6 April, 1963

◁ 116.
The Leighton Buzzard to Dunstable
push-and-pull arrives at Dunstable North,
propelled by a 2-6-2T. Notice the driver
sitting in the front controlling the train,
while the fireman stays on the foot-
plate to fire the loco when propelling.
The passenger service was withdrawn
on 2 July, 1962 and the freight on
3 April, 1967.

12 August, 1961

118.
Farthinghoe, the first station out on the
line from Banbury to Buckingham, painted
in faded red and cream, the BR regional
colours. This original station is certainly
unusual in design and very little brick has
been used in the construction.

119.
Luffenham Junction, with Class 2 2-6-2T
No 41212 arriving with the 12.38 Seaton
to Stamford. The line closed to all traffic
from Market Harborough to Luffenham
on 6 June, 1966.

11 September, 1965

120.
Verney Junction was the point where the
Metropolitan and Great Central Railways'
Joint line from Aylesbury joined up with
the LNWR Oxford to Cambridge line.
Here Ivatt Class 2 2-6-2T No 41275
stands at Verney Junction with the
Buckingham to Bletchley push-and-pull
working in 1959. Oxford to Bletchley
and Bedford to Cambridge closed to passengers on 1 January, 1968. The same
date also saw the complete closure of the
section from Goldington to Cambridge.

121 and 122.
Banbury Merton Street, the LNWR
terminus in the town, just across the road
from the GWR station, closed to passengers on 2 January, 1961. The upper picture shows the whole station with overall
roof, minus glass, and the lower picture
shows the interior—a piece of untouched
Victoriana.

BANBURY.

123 and 124. (*Above*) Piddington, showing the Midland signal box, lamps and fencing, although the signal posts are BR. (*Below*) Olney, also on the Bedford to Northampton branch of the former Midland Railway; the junction for the former Stratford-on-Avon & Midland Junction Railway was between Piddington and Olney at Ravenstone Wood. Freight services over this line were withdrawn on 28 June, 1958. On the Bedford to Northampton branch the passenger service ceased on 5 March, 1962 and freight to Piddington from Oakley Junction on the Midland main line ceased on 6 January, 1964.

125. The 15.30 Peterborough East to Northampton arrives at Oundle hauled by a Class 5 2-6-0. The passenger service from Peterborough to Northampton was withdrawn on 4 May, 1964 and Peterborough to Rugby on 6 June, 1966. Oundle to Thrapston closed to all traffic on 4 May, 1964 and Oundle to Peterborough on 6 November, 1972. The Market Harborough line closed to all traffic from Yarwell Junction and Kingscliffe on 3 June, 1968. Wansford to Orton Waterville is now part of the growing preserved Nene Valley Railway.

11 April, 1964

126. Turvey, another station on the former Midland Railway Bedford to Northampton branch prior to closure to passenger traffic on 5 March, 1962. The line from Northampton to Piddington is still open to Piddington Ordnance Depot, operated by the army.

Gloucestershire, Avon and South Wales

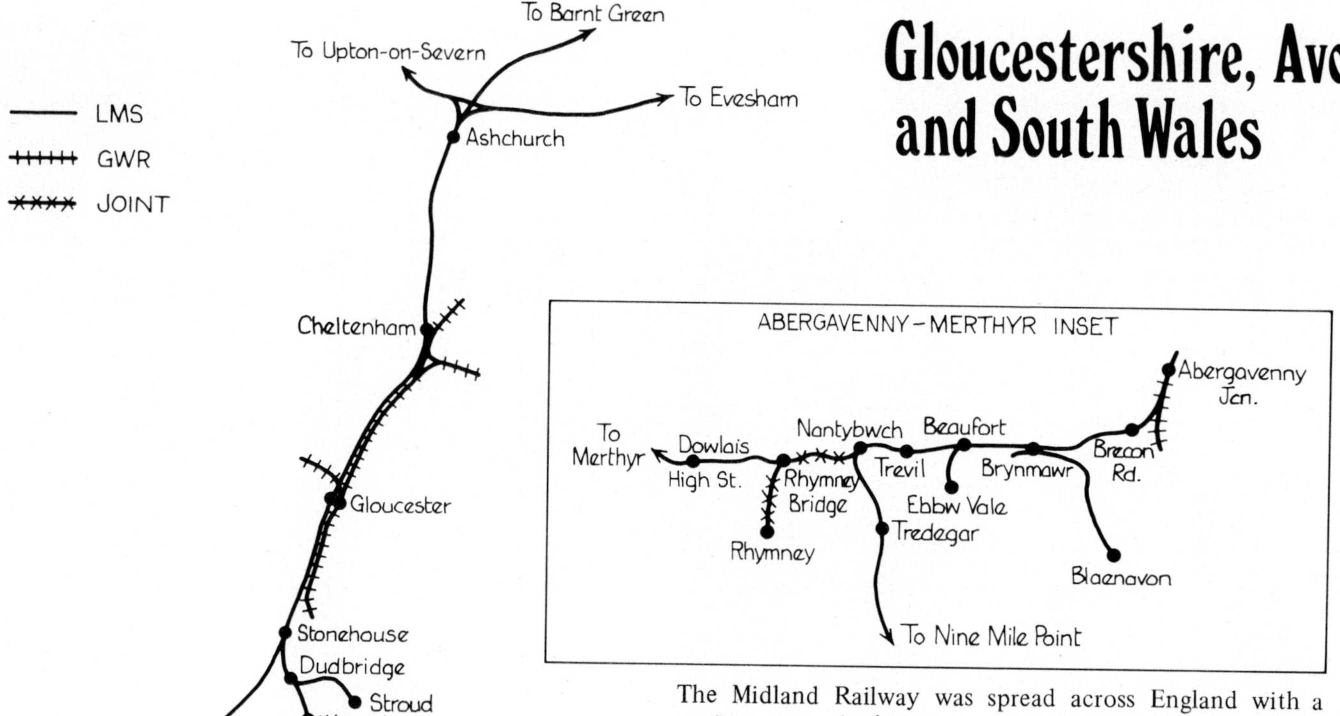

The Midland Railway was spread across England with a route system similar to an enormous 'K' with Gloucestershire at the bottom. The Midland, apart from penetration to Bristol and Bournemouth, spread to South Wales via Hereford & Brecon and the Neath & Brecon Railway over which it had running powers. The LNWR had access to South Wales via the North & West line from Shrewsbury and had the Abergavenny to Merthyr line which connected all the South Wales valley lines, enabling the LNWR to tap the lucrative coal traffic—much to the annoyance of the Great Western.

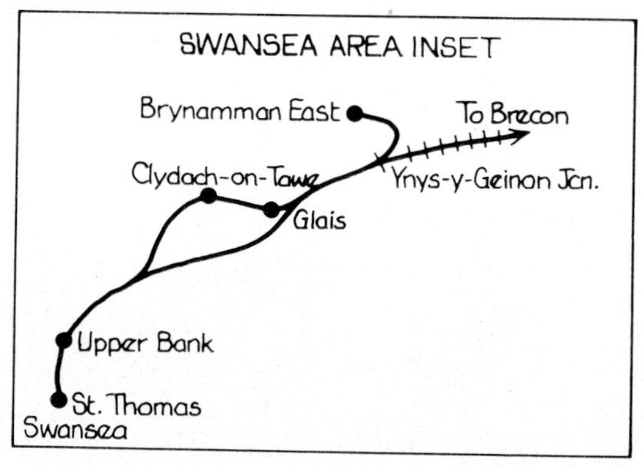

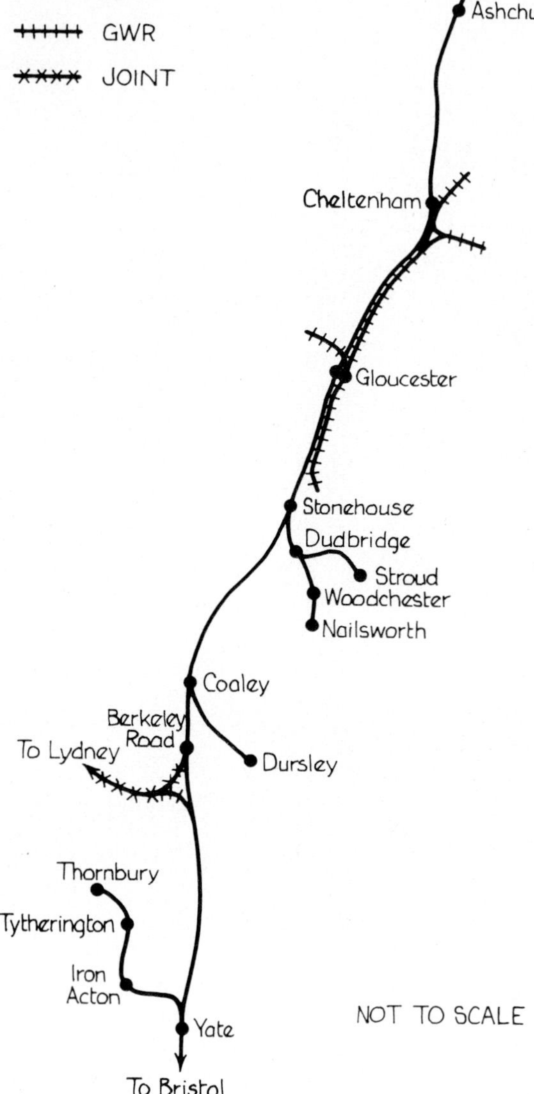

127. Nailsworth station buildings which lost their passenger ▷ service on 8 June, 1949, the line closing to freight on 1 June, 1966. The passenger station was out of use as the goods yard was on a different level. One or two railtours went to Nailsworth station after closure, but the platform was festooned with wild flowers. In this picture the passenger station is still inhabited, now alas the building is empty and in a very poor state of repair, being completely overgrown by trees.

16 March, 1962

128. Stroud Wallbridge, the Midland station in town, which ▷ also closed on 8 June, 1949. Freight services were similarly withdrawn on 1 June, 1966; the building still stands.

16 March, 1962

129.
Stonehouse Bristol Road, the branch platforms for Nailsworth and Stroud were separate from the main station, which was some distance away behind the trees.

130.
Dudbridge was the junction for the Stroud Midland branch and Nailsworth. The station is still complete, being painted in the LMS livery, complete with lamps, gates and garden—the inhabitant is the former stationmaster. The platforms have been filled in, and the track has been removed.

16 March, 1962

131 and 132. Scenes on the short Gloucestershire branch line to Thornbury
with a LMS Class 4F 0-6-0 in evidence. (*Above*) The daily goods at Iron
Acton, one of the intermediate stations. (*Below*) The train at Thornbury with
the '4F' taking water. The passenger service ceased on 19 June, 1944 and
freight finished on 3 September, 1967 but Yate to Tytherington Quarry
reopened on 3 July, 1972 for stone traffic.

(Both) 15 March, 1962

133 and 134. (*Above*) On 16 July, 1953 the branch train for Dursley waits at Coaley with No 41748, a Midland half cab side tank, a Johnson 0-6-0T of 1878 classified 1F. (*Below*) Arrival at Dursley on 5 July, 1947 with a Midland '1F' 0-6-0T. The passenger service was withdrawn on 10 September, 1962, freight finishing on 13 July, 1970.

135 and 136.

Last days on the Abergavenny to Merthyr line of the former LNWR. The line crossed the 'heads of the valleys' and joined up the various valley lines enabling the LNWR to extract the coal traffic from South Wales to the North. The line ran over some hilly country. (*above*) Abergavenny Brecon Road on 5 January, 1958 and, (*below*) Nantybwch showing the LNWR bridge plate, enamel advertisements, and LNWR lower quadrant signal in 1952. The line closed to all traffic from 6 January, 1958, although Nantybwch to Beaufort remained open for freight until 5 November, 1959.

137 and 138.
(*Above*) Clydach Halt looking east in 1949 showing the low platforms and LNWR lamps. (*Below*) The Ebbw Vale terminus of the LNWR with the last train on 5 January, 1958. The nameboard is painted in the LMS colours of black on a yellow background. Most of the nameboards on the Abergavenny to Merthyr line were still in this form. The regular passenger service to Ebbw Vale ceased on 5 February, 1951—freight finished on 5 November, 1959. The other LNWR branch in the area, that to Blaenavon, closed to freight on 24 June, 1954 and to passengers on 5 May, 1941.

139.
Llandilo to Carmarthen was another out-post of the LNWR in South Wales. Here a GWR pannier tank stops at Nantgaredig with an all stations train from Carmarthen. Note LMS colours on nameboard, black on yellow, and LNWR signal.

8 August, 1962

140.
Tredegar station on the LNWR Sirhowy Valley line which closed to passengers on 13 June, 1960 from Nantybwch. Tredegar to Sirhowy closed to all traffic on 4 November, 1963, Pontllanfraith to Tredegar on 30 April, 1969 and Roger-stone North to Pontllanfraith on 4 May, 1970.

13 July, 1958

GENTLEMEN
GOLDEN GROVE
GROVE POST OFFICE

◁ 141 and 142. Llandilo to Carmarthen stations again.
(*Above*) Golden Grove station with the signalman
holding out the staff for the crew of the arriving pannier
tank. The station was also the local post office. (*Below*)
Drysllwyn platform with the train departing in the background. The branch closed to all traffic on 9 September,
1963.

(Both) 8 August, 1962

143. Llandilo Bridge a year before closure, with a short stopping train from
Carmarthen and a GWR engine. This came about as a result of regional
boundary changes, the Western Region having 'Great Westernised' some of
the ex LMS lines. Another curious branch line owned by the LNWR in
South Wales was that to Llanmorlais, closed completely on 2 September,
1957 having closed to passengers on 5 January, 1931.

8 August, 1962

144 and 145. The Midland Railway also got to South Wales and seen here are views of Midland Railway relics. The top picture shows Clydach-on-Tawe closed to passengers on 25 September, 1950. The lower picture shows a Midland box at Ynis y Geinon, the junction for the Brecon line.

(Both) 15 September, 1962

146 and 147. (*Above*) The small cramped ▷ station at Brynamman East. Note the Midland Railway notice and GWR signal as the other station at Brynamman West is through the arch on the right. (*Below*) Brynamman in LMS days with an 0-6-0 tank on a Swansea train. The service was withdrawn on 25 September, 1950—freight services were withdrawn on 28 September, 1964.

7481

LADIES
WAITING ROOM

Hertfordshire and London

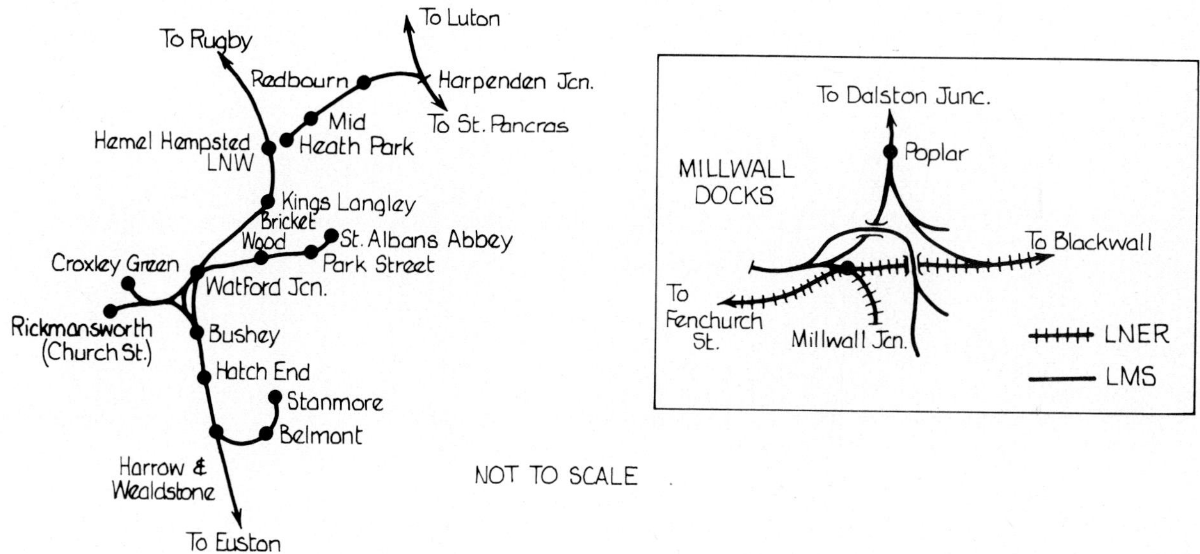

The LMS had country branch lines in the London area which were engulfed by suburbia as the city expanded. The North London Railway and LNWR and MR (North & South Western Junction Joint) had a branch line to Hammersmith & Chiswick from Acton, worked by steam railmotors. This line lost its passenger service in 1916, succumbing to tramway competition. Branch lines to Stanmore and Rickmansworth were originally country branch lines but were outmoded by more modern rivals of the Metropolitan Railway.

148.   Fowler 0-6-0T Class 2F 0-6-0T No 47164 takes water ▷ from a rather leaky bag at Millwall Junction. The Fowler dock tanks were built in 1928 and were a small and fairly rare class of 10, with short wheel base and outside cylinders, designed to negotiate the sharp curves of the dockland areas. The other end of the NLR system saw the short branch to Hammersmith & Chiswick (NSWJ) closed to freight on 3 May, 1965 having closed to passengers in 1916.

28 February, 1957

151 and 152.
Scenes on the St Albans Abbey branch in April 1958. (*Above*) Stanier 0-4-4T No 41901, and of a class of 10, working a special and crossing the four wheeled railbus at Bricket Wood. (*Right*) Inside the terminus at St Albans Abbey with its overall roof can be seen the experimental four wheeled railbus which only lasted until replaced by more conventional standard stock.

◁ 149 and 150.
Millwall Junction, the preserve of the North London Railway 0-6-0Ts. (*Above*) No 58857 with the Poplar to Dalston Junction section of the North London Railway in the background, closed to passengers on 15 May, 1944. (*Below*) No 58859 works an L.C.G.B. railtour at Millwall Junction, a Great Eastern station, although used by Midland trains to Poplar Goods. An example of the 1879 Park 0-6-0Ts, No 58850, is preserved at Sheffield Park on the Bluebell Railway, Sussex.

(Both) 5 May, 1956

153.
A special train headed by a Johnson Class 3F 0-6-0 traversing the Midland Hemel Hempstead branch, stops at Redbourne. The branch closed to passengers on 16 June, 1947 from Heath Park Halt to Harpenden. Hemel Hempstead Midland Road, as BR called the branch, closed to freight traffic on 1 July, 1963 and from Claydale Siding to Harpenden on 29 April, 1968.

11 May, 1957

154.
Rickmansworth Church Street, once on the electrified suburban system and abandoned on 2 January, 1967. The passenger service was withdrawn on 3 March, 1952. The companion branch, however, is still open to Croxley Green.

15 August, 1951

155.
Rickmansworth Church Street on 25 August, 1951 with a
three coach multiple unit set of LNWR origin. Note the two
conductor rails, similar to London Transport practice.

156.
Watford Junction with the St Albans branch train, formed
of the experimental four wheeled diesel unit, waiting in
the bay platform on 16 May, 1957.

157 and 158. The upper picture shows Stanmore station buildings and the short canopy in 1958, prior to the arrival of an RCTS tour hauled by Stanier 0-4-4T No 41901. The bottom picture shows the station in LNWR days displaying all the enamel advertisements so beloved of the Edwardians. The line closed to passengers on 15 September, 1952 to Belmont and on 5 October, 1964 to Harrow & Wealdstone. Freight finished from Belmont to Stanmore on 6 July, 1964 and on 5 October, 1964 from Harrow & Wealdstone to Belmont.

159.
The Midland Railway in dockland showing the Poplar Midland Goods branch and evidence of MR architecture. The Great Eastern Poplar station on the Blackwall branch is to the left of the Midland building. Photo taken on 26 July, 1958.

160.
The locos of dockland, the North London tanks, were used to shunt in the restricted sidings. Here No 58857 takes a rest at Millwall Junction in 1956.

Index